D1404731

SPY∙∙ UNIVERSITY ™

The Spy's Guide to Scouting and Reconnaissance

BY Jim **Wiese** **WITH** H. Keith **Melton**

SPY EXPERT

SCHOLASTIC INC.

NEW YORK   TORONTO   LONDON   AUCKLAND   SYDNEY
MEXICO CITY   NEW DELHI   HONG KONG   BUENOS AIRES

CAMERA

**Pigeons were among the world's first
aerial photographers. Turn to page 44
to find out more about this!**

ISBN 0-439-33647-3

Copyright © 2003 by Scholastic Inc.

Editor: Andrea Menotti
Designers: Robert Rath, Lee Kaplan
Illustrations: Daniel Aycock

Photos:
page 21 (both photos), courtesy of ghilliesuits.com; page 24, courtesy of Custom Concealment; pages 29, 31, and 32,
aerial photos by AirPhoto USA; page 30, U.S. Navy and Coast Guard photos; page 44 (bottom), NASA photo by Jim Ross; page 46 (top),
NASA photo by Judson Brohmer; page 46 (center), U.S. Air Force photo; page 46 (bottom), U.S. Air Force photo by George Rolmaller.
All other photos: www.spyimages.net.

All rights reserved. Published by Scholastic Inc. No part of this publication may be reproduced, stored in
a retrieval system, or transmitted in any form or by any means, electronic, mechanical, photocopying, recording,
or otherwise, without the prior written permission of the publisher. For information regarding permission,
write to Scholastic Inc., Attention: Permissions Department, 557 Broadway, New York, NY 10012.

SCHOLASTIC, SPY UNIVERSITY, and associated logos are trademarks and/or registered trademarks of Scholastic Inc.

12 11 10 9 8 7 6 5   4 5 6 7 8/0

Printed in the U.S.A.

First Scholastic printing, May 2003

The publisher has made every effort to ensure that the activities in this book are safe when done as instructed.
Children are encouraged to do their spy activities with willing friends and family members and to respect others'
right to privacy. Adults should provide guidance and supervision whenever the activity requires.

CECIL COUNTY
PUBLIC LIBRARY
301 Newark Ave.
Elkton, MD 21921

FEB 0 1 2006

TABLE OF Contents

👀 This means you'll use your **Spy Gear** in this activity.

🖥 This means you can find a related activity on the **Spy University** web site.

H ere's the situation: Your family's thinking of having a big reunion at Memorial Park. The problem? No one knows much about the park, and you'll need a LOT of info to plan such a big event. For example:

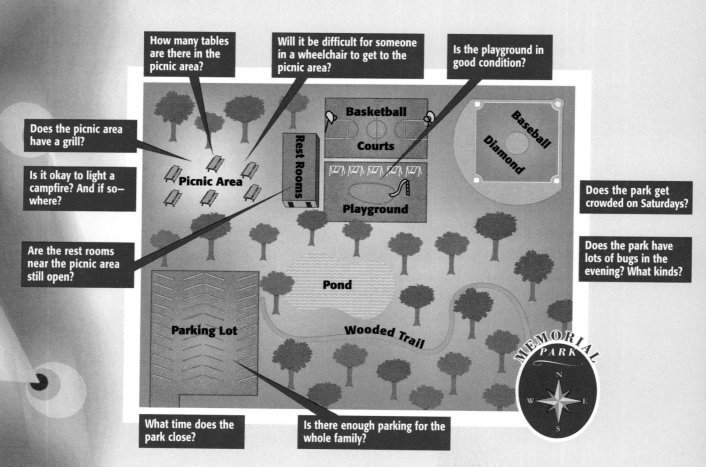

How many tables are there in the picnic area?

Will it be difficult for someone in a wheelchair to get to the picnic area?

Is the playground in good condition?

Does the picnic area have a grill?

Is it okay to light a campfire? And if so— where?

Are the rest rooms near the picnic area still open?

Does the park get crowded on Saturdays?

Does the park have lots of bugs in the evening? What kinds?

What time does the park close?

Is there enough parking for the whole family?

Basketball Courts

Baseball Diamond

Rest Rooms

Picnic Area

Playground

Pond

Parking Lot

Wooded Trail

MEMORIAL PARK

This is a perfect opportunity to try out the new spy skills you'll be learning in *The Spy's Guide to Scouting and Reconnaissance*. This month, you'll learn how spies gather information about a *place*.

IT OUT!

In the case of Memorial Park, you can consult maps and visit the park at various times to get the facts you need. These are techniques spies use, too, when they have easy access to a place. But when spies need to get information about *enemy* territory that they *can't* easily enter, some different techniques and technology come into play.

And *that's* what you'll find in this month's guide. You'll get acquainted with night scopes, parachutes, submarines, spy planes, spy satellites, and even spy *pigeons* (see the Spy Feature for more on this)! But wait—before you gear up and head out into enemy territory, let's tackle some basic questions.

WHAT ARE SCOUTING AND RECONNAISSANCE, EXACTLY?

The words **"scouting"** and **"reconnaissance"** mean pretty much the same thing: an exploratory survey of a location and what's happening there. You've probably heard of "scouting out" a place. "Reconnaissance" comes from a French word that means "to be familiar with." It's often called "recon" (REE-con) or "recee" (REE-see) for short.

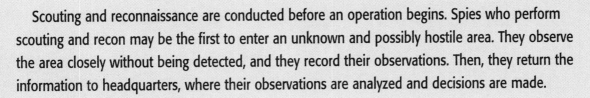

Scouting and reconnaissance are conducted before an operation begins. Spies who perform scouting and recon may be the first to enter an unknown and possibly hostile area. They observe the area closely without being detected, and they record their observations. Then, they return the information to headquarters, where their observations are analyzed and decisions are made.

The information gathered by a recon team is critical to the success of a mission. It may be up to the recon team, for example, to discover the location of important documents inside a building, to observe the movements of guards outside a facility, or to provide a map showing where weapons are kept inside an enemy base. All of this information is used to put together a successful plan of action.

HOW ARE SCOUTING AND RECONNAISSANCE DONE?

Here are some basic scouting and recon techniques:

■ **Use maps.** Spies need to know how to use maps to their advantage. **Operation A1 B2 C3** on page 26 will teach you the ABCs of map maneuvers.

■ **Make maps.** Spies also need to *make* maps and sketches to record their observations. They might also have to *disguise* their maps if they need to sneak them out of enemy territory. Turn to **Operation Picture This** on page 33 to find out more.

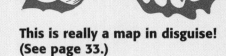

■ **Set up a forward observation post (F.O.P.).** From a hidden observation post, a spy can observe and record information about a specific location and what goes on there. For example, if the spy keeps

This is really a map in disguise! (See page 33.)

watch on a building, he can find out the number of people that enter each day, the kinds of vehicles that move in and out, and what sorts of deliveries are made. This information can help reveal the real purpose of the building (whether it's a factory that's making shoes or *weapons*, for example). Turn to page 11 to set up on your own recon F.O.P.!

■ **Spy by night.** By scouting under cover of darkness, a spy can avoid being seen. To work on your night vision, try **Operation Spy by Night** on page 15.

■ **Drop in!** Spies can parachute into an area, gather the information they need, then quietly sneak out. **Operation Oh 'Chute!** on page 18 will introduce you to the basics of falling safely from the sky.

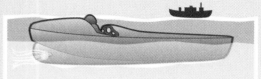

■ **Float in!** Spies can slip among ships using one-person submarines. See **Operation Undersea Spy** on page 36 for more on this.

■ **Spy from the sky.** Much can be discovered by analyzing photos taken by spy planes and satellites. **Operation Spies in Space** on page 28 will give you the *overview*!

ABOUT THIS MONTH'S SPY GEAR

It's tough to scout without the right equipment, so you've been issued a Day/Night Spy Scope for this month's operations.

■ During the day, your Spy Scope can be used from an observation post to help you get a close-up view of your target. Turn the focus wheel until you see a clear, crisp image.

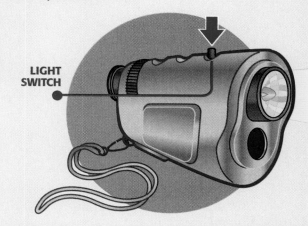

LIGHT SWITCH

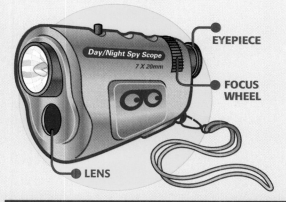

Day/Night Spy Scope
7 X 20mm

EYEPIECE

FOCUS WHEEL

LENS

■ At night, you can use the night-scope function to see in the dark. Just click on the light using the button on top.

ABOUT THIS MONTH'S WEB SITE

You'll have access to a whole new training session this month on the Spy University web site (**www.scholastic.com/spy**). It's got all kinds of scouting and reconnaissance challenges! So, grab your new password and get on-line!

the password spot

Shhhh. This month's web site password is
scoutview

A word to wise spies

● Sometimes (we'll tell you when), you'll need to have a senior spy (an adult) with you when you perform your spy mission.

● Do these activities with your friends and family, in safe places. That means no solo scouting, and no scouting in places you don't already know to be safe.

This Russian monocular (a mini telescope) folds down to a small size, making it easy to hide and carry.

SPY TALK

Here are this month's spy terms. Review them now, and come back here later whenever you need a refresher. You'll find these words in **boldface** throughout the book.

▼ **Aerial:** From the sky (as in *aerial reconnaissance* or *aerial photo*).

▼ **Astrolabe:** A measuring device that uses angles and distances to determine the height of buildings, trees, and other tall things. (Pronounced AS-truh-layb.)

▼ **Camouflage:** To disguise something by making it blend in with its surroundings.

▼ **Carrier pigeon:** A pigeon that delivers messages.

▼ **Cipher:** A form of code in which the letters of a message are replaced with a new set of letters or numbers according to some rule.

▼ **Code:** A system designed to hide the meaning of a message by substituting letters, numbers, words, symbols, sounds, or signals in place of the actual text.

▼ **Forward observation post (F.O.P.):** A safely hidden spot behind (or near) enemy lines from which a spy can make observations.

▼ **Ghillie suit:** A special camouflage outfit with natural materials (like branches or leaves) attached to help a spy blend in with nature. ("Ghillie" is pronounced GIL-ee.)

▼ **Infiltrate:** To sneak into a restricted area.

▼ **Key:** A chart that explains the symbols on a map.

▼ **Landmark:** An obvious object or place used as a reference to help you locate something.

▼ **Map reference:** A way to specify a location on a map using a letter and a number.

▼ **Monocular:** A device for seeing into the distance, like binoculars, but for one eye.

▼ **Reconnaissance:** An exploratory survey of an unfamiliar place. (Pronounced re-CON-uh-sahns.)

▼ **Scouting:** See **reconnaissance**.

▼ **Spy network:** A group of spies who work together toward a common goal.

▼ **Target:** The object of surveillance.

These Israeli night-vision goggles were used by the CIA for surveillance during the 1980s.

T SAVE THE rees!

SPYquest It's Saturday and the weather is great. You're on your way to Cold Creek Park for a meeting with your spy network.

Cold Creek Park is one of your favorite places. There's a creek, of course, but there's also a playground, a soccer field, and a small forest with a walking trail. Your spy network likes to meet in a small clearing in the forest. It's a perfect spot—easy to find, but far enough away from the trail that you won't be seen or overheard. The spot was discovered by Sam, your network's scouting and recon specialist. Sam lives right on the edge of the forest and thinks of it as part of his own backyard.

As you're approaching the forest, you're surprised to see Sam coming toward you. He looks upset.

"What's wrong?" you ask. "Isn't the meeting *that* way?"

"It is," Sam says. "But wait till you see *this*."

You follow Sam to the edge of the forest, and you immediately see what he's

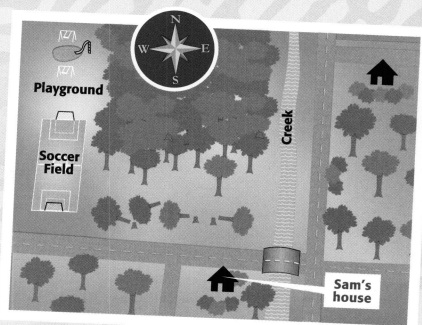

upset about. Four trees have been cut down and left lying on the ground.

"It must have happened yesterday," Sam says, "because I know this mess wasn't here yesterday morning when I left for school. I didn't get home till after dark, so I can't say exactly when it happened. Looks like someone came through here with a chain saw."

"Why would someone do this?" you ask.

"I don't know," Sam says. "My dad says they might be planning on cutting down all the trees and building houses or an apartment building."

"*What?* They can't do that. It's a *park*," you say.

"My dad says the forest isn't really part of the park. It's someone's private property," Sam says. "I'm not sure whose, though."

"I'm sure we can find out," you say. "But first, let's get the rest of the network."

You head over to the meeting place and find Liz, Zoe, and Jeff already there. You explain what's going on, and everyone agrees that the first step is to split up and search the forest for other cut-down trees. After everyone has searched and reported back, it's clear that only the trees on the edge of the forest were cut down.

"Now we have to figure out who did this and why," you say.

Everyone has suggestions for your next step, but two of them sound best.

Liz thinks you should check the records at City Hall to find out who owns the property and if any development plans are underway. Sam wants to set up an observation post near the forest, with a view of the road. He thinks whoever did this might come back to cut down more trees.

Liz, Zoe, and Jeff are busy this afternoon, so it's just going to be you and Sam. Which one of the ideas will you tackle first?

This is your Spy Quest for this month. Choose your path wisely! If you hit a dead end, you'll have to back up and choose another path!

■ If you decide to check the records at City Hall, turn to **page 17**.

■ If you decide to set up an observation post, turn to **page 14**.

OPERATION Super SCOUT

1

A spy on a **recon** mission behind enemy lines needs to find a safely hidden spot from which he can make his observations. This is called a **forward observation post (F.O.P.)**. You learned about two kinds of observation posts in your *Trainee Handbook*—fixed and mobile. An F.O.P. is a kind of fixed observation post, but since it involves being inside (or close to) enemy territory, it's called a *forward* observation post.

> ### STUFF YOU'LL NEED
> - 👓 Spy Scope
> - Notebooks
> - Pencils
> - Watches
>
> ### YOUR NETWORK
> - A friend to challenge you in a match of recon skills

Spies set up F.O.P.'s to keep watch on a *place*. For example, a spy might set up an F.O.P. near an enemy military facility and record the number and kind of trucks that enter and exit.

It's not easy to set up an F.O.P. First, the spy has to sneak into an area he knows little about. Then, he has to scout around for the best possible spot for watching without being seen. A really great F.O.P. provides cover, but it also gives the spy a good view of his **target**. The F.O.P. doesn't have to be right *next* to the target, though, because spies can use special equipment, like the Spy Scope you got this month, to see things from far away.

So, if you're ready start your first recon mission, grab your Spy Scope, and let's move *forward*!

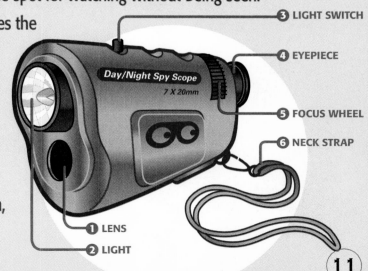

Day/Night Spy Scope
7 X 20mm

3 LIGHT SWITCH
4 EYEPIECE
5 FOCUS WHEEL
6 NECK STRAP
1 LENS
2 LIGHT

SPYmissions

WHAT YOU DO

Are you a Super Scout? You'll know for sure when you and a friend finish this operation. You'll start by deciding what you're going to observe, and why. Then, you'll each set up your own F.O.P., make your observations, and compare notes. The best observer wins the title of Super Scout!

1 Work together to decide what place you'll observe, and a reason for your observations. For example, you may decide to observe your school (before or after school hours) to determine where delivery trucks arrive, what they bring, and how the deliveries are unloaded.

2 Split up. You and your friend will observe the same place, but you'll choose different locations for your F.O.P.'s. You'll also have different equipment. Since your friend won't have a Spy Scope, he'll have to make do without. Or, if he happens to have his own spy gear, he can bring that (to be fair).

3 Plan your F.O.P. First, you'll need to find the right spot. Remember—you need to see without being seen. If you want to watch trucks deliver goods to your school, you'll need an F.O.P. with a good view of the loading dock. If the truck driver can see you, though, the spot isn't secret. Can you find a tree, a large rock, or a building that provides good cover?

4 Put together your recon kit. Include your Spy Scope, a notebook, a pencil, and a watch. You'll also need **camouflage** (clothing that helps you to blend in with your surroundings).

5 Plan secret routes for getting in and out of your F.O.P. If you're observing a school, you'll need to stay out of the way of kids and teachers!

Was that an elephant going down the road? In Vietnam, the answer was sometimes…yes!

During the Vietnam War (1964–1975), spies for the American military kept an eye on the roads. Instead of using paper to record observations, the spies used "elephant transmitters."

The elephant transmitter had buttons on it with pictures of different types of transport. If the spy saw a truck, he pushed the truck button once. If he saw three jeeps, he pushed the jeep button three times. If he saw an elephant pass by, he pushed the elephant button. This picture-based system worked well, since it could be used by anyone, no matter what language he spoke.

Each day, an airplane flew over the spy's location to collect his information. Electronic equipment in the plane contacted the elephant transmitter, and the transmitter's data was uploaded to the plane. It was a safe way to transfer information without making direct contact.

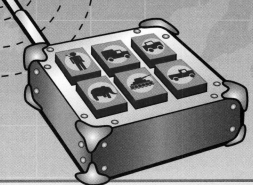

6 Get out there and scout! Observe everything you can. For example, how many trucks arrive? When do they arrive? How big are they? What color are they? Do they have markings? What are their license plate numbers? How many people are driving them? What are the people wearing? Does someone help them unload? Who? You can write down your info and make a sketch to show what the trucks look like.

F.O.P. Location Alpha

Time	Observations
1430hrs	Truck with 3 people delivers strange heavy boxes. B&D Foods
1445hrs	Lunch lady drags 4 big garbage bags to dumpster.
1500hrs	Stray cat walks by, stops to sniff empty milk carton.

7 Make your getaway—secretly.

8 Meet your friend and compare notes. How much info did you gather? How much info did your friend gather? Which one of you is the Super Scout?

9 Analyze your info. What did you learn about your school that you didn't know before? Did you find out anything about the plans your school has for lunches, events, or sports?

MORE FROM HEADQUARTERS

1 Use your Spy Scope to read license plate numbers on cars. How far away can you be and still read the numbers? How much can you see at night, when you use the Spy Scope's light?

SPY STATE
BNV · 3406

SPY STATE
BNV · 3406

2 Set up a secret F.O.P. Then, let a friend know what you're watching (tell him your target—like your school). Can your friend see you from the target location? If he can, try again—this time making your F.O.P. less visible.

WHAT'S THE SECRET?

Your Spy Scope is really a **monocular**. That's binoculars made for—you've got it!—one eye! Monoculars are basically the same thing as telescopes. They help you see distant objects more clearly.

Your eyes have trouble seeing faraway objects because the light bouncing off of them is too dim, and the objects appear very small. If you had a bigger eye, it could gather more light and see the objects more clearly. That's basically what a monocular does. It acts like a big eye and collects more light from faraway objects than your eyes can.

Your Spy Scope uses two lenses and two mirrors to help you see into the distance.

The first lens gathers the light bouncing off of faraway objects and collects it in one spot, creating an enlarged, upside-down image of the object. Two mirrors flip the image right side up again, and reflect the image to the second lens. The second lens magnifies the image again so you can see it even more clearly.

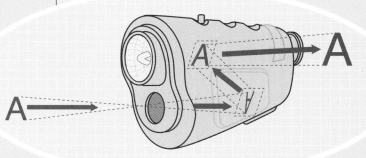

(continued from page 10)

You decide that Sam has the right idea, so you rush back to his house to set up an observation post.

After scouting out the area, you decide that the best place for the observation post is behind a bush in Sam's yard. This gives you a view of both roads that run along the sides of the forest. You also have a good view of the area where the trees were cut down. You have your Spy Scope with you, so you can get a closer look if necessary.

You and Sam take turns at the post, making sure that the area is watched all afternoon. By the end of the afternoon, you compare notes. Between the two of you, you've seen a bunch of cars go by and some people entering the forest to walk along the trail, but you *haven't* seen anything suspicious.

"I think I've had enough for today," you say.

But then you both look up. A large truck drives by and pulls over right in front of the cut-down trees! A tall man gets out of the truck and looks at the trees, shaking his head.

You use your Spy Scope to read the writing on the truck's door. It says Big Al's Tree Service, and there's a phone number below it. You quickly jot down the number in your log.

"Come on," Sam says. "Let's go talk to him."

"Wait," you say. "Let's just watch and see what he does. We can always call him later if we need to talk to him."

"I think we should talk to him *now*," Sam says. "We've been waiting all day for something to happen. Now you want to wait *more*?"

Well, what's it going to be?

- If you decide to approach the man from Big Al's Tree Service, turn to **page 38**.
- If you decide to wait and see what develops, turn to **page 41**.

2

OPERATION SPY BY Night

On dark, moonless nights, spies can sneak into a location, collect the information they need, and slip away unseen. There's only one problem: It's dark! So how can the spies see to collect their info—without falling into holes, crashing into tables, or whacking their shins? The answer is great equipment.

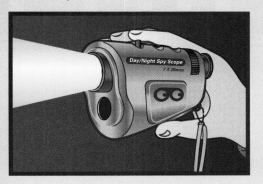

You already know how well your Spy Scope works in daylight. Now it's time to give it a workout in the dark!

STUFF YOU'LL NEED

- **Five different objects to locate**
- **Watch**
- 👓 **Spy Scope**
- **Notebook**

YOUR NETWORK

- **A friend to place objects for you**

WHAT YOU DO

In this operation, you'll use your Spy Scope to find objects hidden in a dark room.

Note: It's best to do this operation at night. However, if you want to do the operation during the day, find a room that's naturally dark or can be darkened easily.

1 Choose five objects that you'll search for with your Spy Scope. Pick objects that are easy to move, and include at least one object that reflects light (like a mirror or a metal spoon).

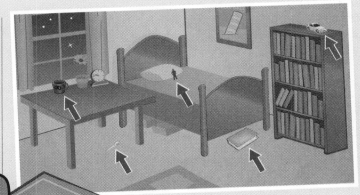

2 Leave the room, and have your friend place the five objects around the room. The objects should be easy to find when you're standing near the door of the room.

3 When your friend is done, have her darken the room. Then, have her start timing you. You'll have five minutes to find all the objects.

4 Now it's your turn. Enter the room, stand in the doorway, and turn on your Spy Scope's light.

5 Look through the Spy Scope and begin searching for the five items. But don't just look around. Instead, scan the room like a real scout. Here's how:

- Start by looking to your left, and scan a line along the highest parts of the room, moving from the left to the right.

- When you reach the right side of the room, slightly lower your field of vision and scan from that point in a line to the left.

- When you are again at a point to your left, again lower your field of vision and scan a line to the right.

- Continue to scan these horizontal lines until you reach the floor.

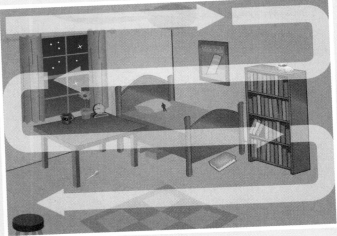

- If you find anything in your scan that seems like it might be one of the objects, stop your scan and look more carefully. If you've definitely found one of the objects, note its location in your notebook.

6 When five minutes are up, stop scanning. How many objects did you find? Which were easiest to find? Where were the objects that you didn't find? How can you improve your scanning techniques?

7 Now switch roles with your friend. Who's faster at finding all the objects?

MORE FROM HEADQUARTERS

If you did a good job finding the hidden objects in this operation, you're ready to move on to the next level. It's time to learn how to find hidden objects *outside*, in the dark. To be safe, you'll need to recruit a senior spy to help you. Ask the senior spy to place five objects (the same ones you used in this operation) in a safe area outside. He can place the objects anywhere—under a bush, beside a flight of steps, or in a doorway. The senior spy should be able to see all the objects from your starting place. Once the senior spy has everything set up, it's your turn. Stand at your starting place, flip on your Spy Scope, and start scanning. Can you find all the objects? Is it harder or easier to find the objects outside?

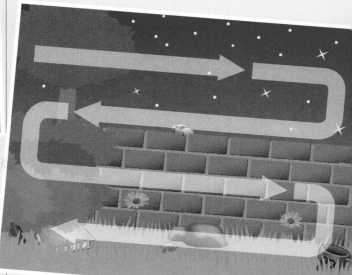

INFRARED VIEWER

INFRARED LIGHT BEAM TRANSMITTER

N9243471

Your Spy Scope uses a flashlight to give you night vision, but that's not the only way to see in the dark. Spies have special night-vision devices that don't cast any visible light at all.

Night-vision devices may work in one of two ways. Some use a technology that collects tiny amounts of light and amplifies it (makes it brighter). Others involve infrared light, which can't be seen by the naked eye. The infrared night-vision device shown on the right sends out an invisible beam of infrared light. By looking through the device's infrared viewer, the user can see the light as it reflects off objects in its path.

The best night-vision devices allow spies to see clearly up to 200 yards (183 m), even in the pitch dark!

This Russian night-vision device uses infrared light that is invisible to the naked eye, but can be seen through the special viewer.

WHAT'S THE SECRET?

When you scan in a pattern, as you did in this operation, you cover the entire search area. That'll help you avoid missing the objects you're looking for. Since a spy's mission depends upon the information gathered through **recon**, it's important to be thorough!

It's much harder to spot stationary objects than *moving* ones. Movement is one of the first things that will catch an observer's eye (that's why you need to stay still when you're hiding!). So, if you were able to succeed in this operation using *still* objects, you know you've got extra-sharp recon skills!

You probably noticed that reflective objects were especially easy to find. That's because the light from your Spy Scope bounced off the mirror or metal and came back to your eyes.

$\mathbb{S}$PYquest

(continued from page 10)

You and Sam go to City Hall and ask where you can get information about the forest on the south side of Cold Creek Park.

You're directed to a room full of maps and records, and the clerk at the desk helps you find the information you need. By looking at copies of old deeds and maps, you discover that the forest has been owned by a family named Franco for generations. The current owner is Julio Franco. You can't find any information about Julio Franco selling or developing the land.

To find out more, you decide you'd better get in touch with Julio Franco.

■ Turn to **page 20** to meet Julio Franco.

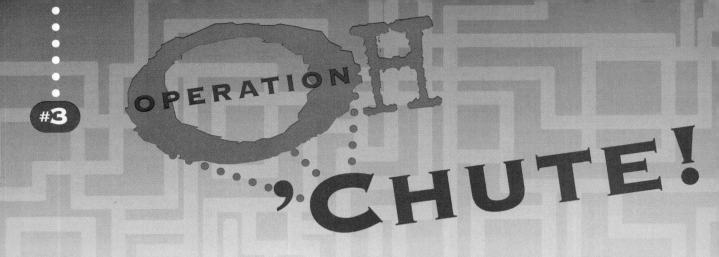

3

OPERATION OH 'CHUTE!

It's a dark night. A plane flies over enemy territory, and out falls a single spy. A few seconds later, a parachute opens, and the spy drifts quietly to the ground. So far, so good! The spy has successfully **infiltrated** (or snuck inside) enemy territory—now he's got to gather the information he needs…and get out!

With the right kind of parachute, a spy can get his **recon** mission off to an extra-stealthy start. But parachutes can come in lots of shapes and sizes. Which kind of parachute works best? And which kind of parachute would *you* choose if you were going to *drop in* on the enemy at night? Try this operation to find out!

STUFF YOU'LL NEED

- **A second-story window or other location about 3 yards (3 m) off the ground**
- **Small plastic action figure (2 to 3 inches [5 to 8 cm] tall)**
- **Scissors**
- **Plastic garbage bag**
- **String**
- **Tape**

YOUR NETWORK

- **A senior spy to join you for this operation**

WHAT YOU DO
PART 1:
JUST 'CHUTE ME!

1 Recruit a senior spy to help you choose a window (or other location) for your parachute drop. The location needs to be about 3 yards (3 meters) off the ground.

2 With your senior spy standing with you at the window, hold the plastic action figure out the window and release it. What happens?

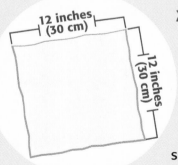

12 inches (30 cm)

12 inches (30 cm)

3 Now you're going to make a parachute for your plastic action figure. To start, cut a 12 x 12-inch (30 x 30-cm) square from the plastic garbage bag.

4 Cut four pieces of string, each 12 inches (30 cm) long.

5 Tape one piece of string to each corner of the plastic square.

6 Tape the other ends of the strings together so they're easier to manage.

7 Tape the strings to the back of the plastic figure.

8 Now you're ready to test out your 'chute! Hold the plastic square near the center so the figure hangs below it.

9 Let go of the 'chute. How does the figure fall *this* time?

PART 2: 'CHUTES GALORE!

Small, square parachutes work pretty well, but what about parachutes of other sizes and shapes? Let's experiment.

1 First, make a *larger* square parachute. Cut an 18 x 18-inch (45 x 45-cm) square from the plastic

18 inches (45 cm)

18 inches (45 cm)

garbage bag. Make the strings 18 inches (45 cm) long as well. Try dropping the plastic figure with *this* parachute. How does this 'chute compare to the first?

2 Rather than making a square parachute, make a *rectangular* parachute that's 8 x 16 inches (20 x 40 cm). Make the strings 16 inches (40 cm) long. How well does the rectangular parachute work compared to the square? Does it float to the ground any differently?

3 Now make a parachute using a *circle* of plastic with a diameter (the distance across the middle of the circle) of 18 inches (45 cm). Tape four 18-inch (45-cm) strings to the edges of the circle, equal distances apart. How well does this shape work?

18 inches (45 cm)

MORE FROM HEADQUARTERS

1 Try making a parachute out of something other than plastic. For example, try making one out of cotton or nylon cloth. Which materials work best?

2 Release your parachute from positions that are lower or higher off the ground. How high does the parachute have to be released so that it has time to fill with air?

WHAT'S THE SECRET?

A parachute slows a person's fall by increasing air resistance—a force that acts against anything that moves through the air. The larger the parachute, the more air resistance it creates, and the slower the fall.

The *shape* of the parachute also affects the way it falls. Square and round parachutes are designed to slow a jumper's fall as much as possible by creating *a lot* of air resistance. But their shape also means that they're strongly affected by winds and air currents.

Rectangular parachutes, on the other hand, are designed to be easy to control. The rectangular shape allows air to escape from beneath the parachute. This means that rectangular parachutes are not as strongly affected by air currents as round and square ones are, and the jumper has more control over both the speed of the fall and the direction the parachute travels. You may have noticed that the square and round parachutes drifted farther from the drop position than the rectangular parachute did. If you want to be able to hit a target with accuracy, a rectangular parachute is the one for you.

Spies also use different-colored parachutes and jump suits (the clothes they wear during a jump) depending on where and when they jump out of the plane. During the day, a white parachute will blend in with the clouds. For a night jump, a dark parachute (and a dark jump suit) will provide good **camouflage**.

(continued from page 17)

You look up Julio Franco's address in the phone book, and you find that he lives just on the other side of the forest. You and Sam head over to see him on your bikes.

You ring the bell and a well-dressed older man answers the door.

"Excuse me, are you Julio Franco?" you ask.

"Yes, I am," he replies. "What can I do for you?"

"We're trying to find out about some trees that were cut down on the other side of the forest. Since you own the forest, we thought you would know why the trees were cut down."

"I'm afraid I don't," Mr. Franco says. "But I did see those trees on my morning walk today. I'm just as confused as you are. I have no idea why anyone would do such a terrible thing."

"So you're not planning to cut down the forest to build houses?" Sam asks.

"Of course not!" Mr. Franco says, looking offended. "I love the forest. When my father transferred the land to me, he made me promise I'd look after it, and I've done just that all these years. I've had many people offer to buy the land over the years, but I've always turned them down."

"Who have you turned down recently?" you ask.

"Well, most recently, I turned down a man named Sal Glover who lives over on the other side of the forest."

"He's my neighbor," Sam says.

"Sal wanted to buy the part of the forest that's across from his house. He said he would put up a playground for the kids in the neighborhood."

"That doesn't sound like something Mr. Glover would do," Sam says. "He doesn't pay any attention to kids."

"Then there was another offer recently from a woman named Marilyn Faulk who owns an ice cream parlor. She said she wanted to buy a strip of the forest so she could put up a snack bar beside the park. I turned her down, too."

So, there are two people who might have wanted the trees cut down—Mr. Glover and Ms. Faulk. Which person should you investigate?

■ If you decide to talk to Mr. Glover, turn to **page 47**.

■ If you decide to talk to Ms. Faulk, turn to **page 31**.

BACK TO NATURE

#4

A spy in a red-and-white striped shirt wouldn't get far in enemy territory. He'd stick out like a sore thumb, and he'd probably get captured before he even *began* his **recon** mission. What would be a better choice of clothing? Anything that would help the spy blend in with his surroundings and make him harder to spot.

A ghillie suit helps this man blend in with the natural environment.

STUFF YOU'LL NEED

- **Clothing for camouflage**
- **Old hat or baseball cap to match your clothing**
- **Clear packing tape**
- **About a dozen safety pins**
- **Shoelaces that match your clothing**
- **Natural materials (like small branches and leaves) or fabric**

YOUR NETWORK

- **A senior spy to help you cut branches**
- **A friend to search for you**

In the natural world, some animals are very good at hiding in plain sight. Moths can look like tree bark, and flounder, a kind of fish, look amazingly like the sand on the ocean floor. This is called **camouflage**, and a good recon spy needs to get in on that game. In this operation, you'll learn about the ultimate camouflage gear: the **ghillie suit**. You'll start by making a ghillie hat, and then you can move on to the whole suit if you're up for it. So, get ready to get back to nature!

A ghillie suit can make a person very hard to spot!

WHAT YOU DO

1 As you did in **Operation Super Scout** on page 11, choose a good spot for a **forward observation post (F.O.P.)**. Your F.O.P. should be located in a safe area like a backyard, a park, or a schoolyard. Be sure your F.O.P. has some features like bushes, tall grass, trees, or large rocks that make it a really good hiding place.

2 Now it's time to suit up in camouflage clothing. Look at the colors around your F.O.P. What color clothing will help you blend in with your surroundings?

3 Once you've got your camouflage clothing together, it's time to make your ghillie hat. Because your head will be the most visible part of your body as you keep watch from your F.O.P., your ghillie hat will be the most important part of your camouflage. To make your ghillie hat, find an old hat (preferably a baseball cap, since they're sturdy) that's one of the colors of your F.O.P.

4 Now get some natural materials from around your F.O.P. that you can attach to the hat. For example, if you're going to hide behind a bush, have a senior spy help you cut several small branches, with leaves, from the bush. If you plan to hide in tall grass, grab some grass. If you're going to hide in an area where there are piles of dead leaves on the ground, collect some dead

leaves. If you want to hide behind a bale of hay, grab a few handfuls of hay. Got the idea?

5 Attach the natural materials to your hat. They should stick out from the hat in several different directions. Your goal is to make your hat look like part of the natural environment, and to hide the shape of your head and shoulders.

You can attach your materials in several ways:

- You can use clear packing tape to stick them on.

- You can use shoelaces to attach the materials. First, cut the shoelaces into shorter pieces. Tie one end of the shoelace to the branch (or other natural item), and then safety pin the other end of the lace to your hat.

- You can also just safety pin some of the materials directly onto your hat.

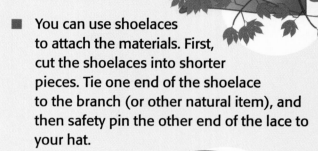

The best way to make your ghillie hat is to use a combination of all three of these methods and to arrange the materials so that they hide the tape and safety pins.

It's also important to let some of the materials hang in front of your face so that they conceal your eyes and mouth (the most visible parts of your face). Be creative in your arrangement!

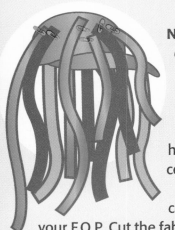

Note: If you can't find enough natural materials (or if a senior spy prefers that you don't use them), you can attach strips of fabric to your hat instead. Use solid-colored fabrics, and choose a few different colors that blend in with your F.O.P. Cut the fabric into thin strips about 1 inch (2.5 cm) wide. Attach these strips to your hat using tape and safety pins, and arrange them so that they hang down in all directions.

6 Now you're ready to test your camouflage. Find a friend to act as the **target** of your surveillance (and make sure he hasn't seen your ghillie hat). Tell your friend that you're going to watch him from an observation post as he moves around a particular area. Challenge him to try and find you. You should be able to see your friend from your F.O.P., but he shouldn't be able to see you! And remember, you only want to observe, not move around and attract attention to yourself. Your ghillie hat will be much more effective if you act like you're part of the landscape—so stay still!

7 How did you do? Did your ghillie hat and camouflage suit make you hard to spot? If your friend found you, ask him how, and see if you can improve your camouflage. If he didn't, way to go!

MORE FROM HEADQUARTERS

Now that you have a ghillie *hat*, try making a whole ghillie *suit*. Attach natural materials from your F.O.P. to your camouflage clothing using tape, safety pins and shoelaces like you used on your hat. Ask another friend to find you now. Does this added camouflage make you harder to spot?

You've probably seen military personnel in clothing that's covered with green, black, and brown splotches. Those outfits are called "camouflage suits," but they're not the same thing as a ghillie suit. The ghillie suit goes one step further.

Ghillie suits *start* with camouflage clothing, and then plant materials or rough fabrics like burlap (which can look like tree bark) are attached to the suit. The idea is to not only blend with the *colors* of the natural environment, but also to change the human *shape* altogether. The plant materials and the fabric add depth to the body, and they blur the outline of the human form. The photo on this page shows you just how well this can work!

This ghillie suit is meant to help its wearer blend in with a woodlands environment. It's made of burlap that has been dyed to match the bark of the trees. As you can see, all parts of the body are covered—even the face.

(continued from page 41)

You decide to call Big Al's Tree Service.

A woman named Nancy answers the phone, and you ask her if Big Al's Tree Service had anything to do with the trees that were cut down in the forest near Cold Creek Park.

"We've never done any work on that forest, especially not the kind you're describing. Sounds like a mess!"

"It is," you say.

"Besides," Nancy says. "Al was working on a landscaping job all day yesterday."

"Do you know why a man from your Tree Service stopped by the forest today?" you ask.

"I have no idea," she says. "Was the man driving a green truck?"

"Yeah," you say.

"That was Al himself. He drives by that forest on his way home from work. Maybe he was just curious like you are. He *is* a tree lover, after all. You can call back Monday and ask him yourself if you want."

"Thanks," you say. "Maybe we will."

■ You *might* call Al on Monday, but for now it looks like this is a dead end. Turn back and try another idea!

JASPER MASKELYNE AND HIS MAGIC GANG

Disguising a *person* with camouflage is one thing, but what about disguising 1,000 tanks? Does that sound tough? Then meet Jasper Maskelyne, a British magician who used crafty illusions to fool the Germans during World War II (1939–1945).

Maskelyne was one of the best magicians in England. When he put his skills to work for the British army, the result was some amazing "military magic" that helped the British and their allies win World War II.

Maskelyne and his team of fellow army men, called the Magic Gang, were in charge of making British forces appear and disappear—as if by magic. One of their most important successes was the Battle of El Alamein in North Africa.

It was 1942, at the height of World War II, and the British were planning a counterattack against German forces in North Africa. The attack was to take place at the northern end of the Germans' front line. If the Germans saw the British gathering their forces to attack, the plan would fail. Somehow, Maskelyne and his Magic Gang had to find a way to disguise the British forces and keep the Germans guessing.

Maskelyne's team started by disguising 1,000 tanks at the northern end of the Germans' front line so they looked like simple supply trucks. Then, 30 miles to the south, the team assembled 2,000 fake tanks, made of cardboard and plywood. The Magic Gang even built a fake railway line, a fake water pipeline, and had fake radio broadcasts and sound effects at their southern site.

The battle at the northern end of the German lines, at El Alamein, began on October 23, 1942. The British trick succeeded in catching the Germans totally off guard. The battle proved to be the turning point in the British campaign against the Germans in North Africa.

The Battle of El Alamein was only *one* of Maskelyne's amazing accomplishments. In 1941, Maskelyne's team created a fake harbor a few miles away from a *real* harbor at Alexandria, Egypt. This site, complete with a fake lighthouse, harbor buildings, and ships, was destroyed by German bombs. The real harbor was unharmed.

Maskelyne's team also used special effects to confuse German bombers. As the bombers flew over North Africa at night, searching for the Suez Canal, they were dazzled by a wheel of spinning lights nine miles across. They couldn't see a thing, and they wound up missing their targets completely. How did Maskelyne do it? With giant searchlights fitted with spinning mirrors!

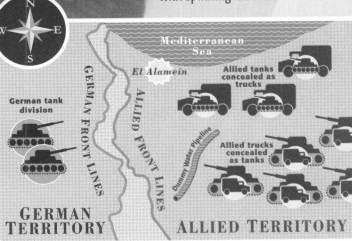

25

5

OPERATION A1 B2 C3

STUFF YOU'LL NEED

- **Four sheets of plain paper**
- **Two rulers**
- **Two pencils**

YOUR NETWORK

- **A friend to play the game**

Maps are very important tools for spies, especially when it comes to **recon**. How do you find what you need on a map? A good place to start is with a **map reference**.

A map reference is a way to specify a location on a map. On many maps, you'll see letters along the top and bottom of the map and numbers along the sides. You can direct someone to any part of the map by providing the right letter and number. For example, to find map location B3, you start at the letter B on top of the map and move down the map until you're directly across from the number 3.

MAP REFERENCE B3

To get some practice using map references, how about playing a game of *Spot the Spy Gear*?

WHAT YOU DO

1 Use your pencil and ruler to make two grids on two separate pages, as shown here. Have your friend do the same. Write "My Gear" above one grid, and write "My Searches" above the other grid.

2 Each of you must place four items of spy gear in the grid marked "My Gear." You each have a camera, a Spy Scope, a codebook, and a

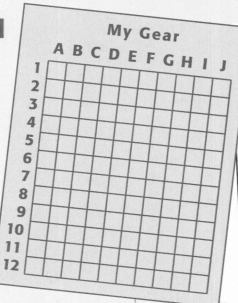

My Gear

My Searches

radio transmitter, and each piece of gear takes up a different number of grid squares, as you can see in the list below. Place your items anywhere you want on the grid marked "My Gear." Don't let your friend see where you're placing your items.

X Camera ■ Place one X in any square to represent a camera.

■ Place two X's in a horizontal or vertical line to represent a Spy Scope.

X X or X / X
Spy Scope

X X X or X / X / X
Codebook

■ Place three X's in a horizontal or vertical line to represent a codebook.

■ Place four X's in a line for a radio transmitter.

X X X X or X / X / X / X
Radio Transmitter

3 Now it's time to play the game. The object of the game is to find where your friend is hiding her spy gear. Take turns searching for one another's gear by calling out a map reference (for example, C5). If your friend has an item in the C5 position, she calls out "hit," and you put an X on that square in your "My Searches" grid. If your friend doesn't have an item at the location you chose, she calls out "miss," and you put an O in the square. Then it's your friend's turn to call out a map reference, and you'll have to tell her whether she hit your gear or missed it.

4 When you or your friend find all the squares that make up an item, that item has been spotted. For example, if you find four hits in a row, you know that you've found your friend's radio transmitter.

5 Take turns until one of you wins by finding all of the other person's spy gear.

MORE FROM HEADQUARTERS

Create your own game of *Spot the Spy Gear*! Think of four new pieces of spy gear that you can hide, and decide how many squares each item will occupy.

WHAT'S THE SECRET?

Map references help you make quick use of a map—and that's important, because often during a recon mission, speed is crucial! Rather than scanning the whole map to find a single location, your eye can go right to the spot you're looking for.

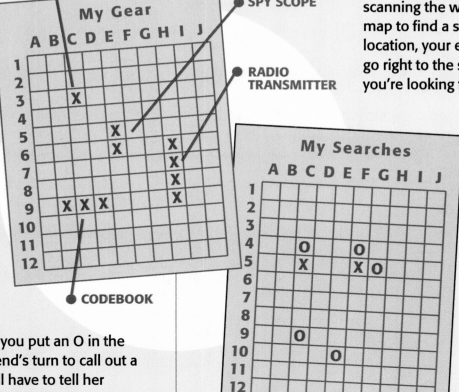

CAMERA
My Gear
SPY SCOPE
RADIO TRANSMITTER
CODEBOOK

My Searches

27

SPIES IN SPACE

#6

With help from satellites and spy planes, spies can get a lot of information about a place without ever actually going there. In fact, by studying photos taken from above, a spy can keep an eye on any number of locations around the world without even leaving her *desk*!

In this operation, you'll be in charge of analyzing some real **aerial** photos. See what it's like to spy from the sky!

STUFF YOU'LL NEED
- **Pencil and paper**

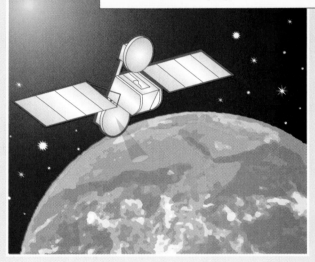

WHAT YOU DO

PART 1:
MYSTERY MONUMENTS

1 Look at the aerial photo on the next page. Can you tell which city it is?

2 Find the following **landmarks**. The answers are on page 48, listed by **map references**.

◎	1. **Washington Monument**	⊞	6. **Rayburn Office Building**
	2. **The Capitol Building**		7. **Reflecting Pool**
◎	3. **Jefferson Memorial**	●	8. **The Ellipse**
●	4. **Hirshorn Museum**		9. **Highway 395 bridge across the Potomac River**
	5. **Union Station (a train station)**		10. **FBI Building**

Photo: AirPhoto USA

A B C D E

1 2 3 4 5 6 7 8 9 10

PART 2:
SHIPS AHOY!

Take a look at the photo on page 31. It's an aerial view of a port in San Diego, California. Using the pictures of navy and coast guard ships below, how many of each kind can you count? Consider size, shape, and markings as you identify each ship. You can check your answers on page 48.

NAME	SHAPE	DESCRIPTION	HOW MANY?
Hospital Ship		This ship carries doctors and nurses who help soldiers and sailors when they're injured.	
Amphibious Ship		This ship carries airplanes, helicopters, and the hovercrafts that marines use when they invade by sea.	
Cruiser		A cruiser provides protection to large ships like aircraft carriers. It shoots down enemy aircraft and fires at targets on land and at sea.	
Destroyer		The destroyer provides protection to large ships like aircraft carriers. It fights enemies in the air, at sea, on land, and underwater.	
Oiler		This ship carries fuel, ammunition, and food for ships while they're at sea.	
Ocean-going Tug		The tug is a powerful boat that tows large ships out to sea and helps them move around.	
Coast Guard Cutter		This ship patrols the waters off our coast and rescues people in danger at sea.	

Photo: AirPhoto USA

(*continued from page 20*)

You pay a visit to Ms. Faulk at her ice cream parlor.

"Oh, yes," she says enthusiastically. "I've been trying to get Mr. Franco to sell me a little strip of land so I can put up a snack bar near the playground. It'd be perfect, don't you think?"

She pulls out a map to show you.

"You see?" she points to the map. "Right here."

You look at Ms. Faulk's map. She's hoping to build her snack bar on the *north* side of the forest, nowhere near the cut trees.

"So you're not interested in this land right here?" Sam asks, pointing to the area where the trees were cut.

"No," she says. "It's really quiet over there. I wouldn't do much business. I want to be where the crowds are!"

■ Sounds like a dead end, all right. Turn back and try again.

CECIL COUNTY
PUBLIC LIBRARY
301 Newark Ave.
Elkton, MD 21921

PART 3: WHAT'S DIFFERENT?

This photo shows the same area you saw on page 31, but with a difference. What has changed? Check your answer on page 48.

Photo: AirPhoto USA (photo modified)

MORE FROM HEADQUARTERS

1 Check the Internet for a satellite picture of your own neighborhood. Go to **www.terraserver.com**.

At the Terraserver site, follow the instructions to find a satellite photo of your home area (by entering your address or clicking on the map). Can you find your house? Can you find other landmarks? Can you find anything you didn't know was there?

2 Visit the Spy University web site (**www.scholastic.com/spy**) for another out-of-this-world challenge with aerial photos.

WHAT'S THE SECRET?

Satellite technology can give you a lot of information about a place. By comparing satellite photos from day to day or week to week, intelligence officers can tell when ships leave a harbor, where tanks are moving, or where new buildings are being constructed.

But what's going on *inside* the buildings? Why are lots of new trucks suddenly showing up at a certain factory? Is the factory *really* manufacturing washing machines—or is it secretly building missiles? When it comes to questions like these, eyes in the sky are no replacement for spies on the ground.

SPYquest

(continued from page 47)

You rush over to Mr. Bascom's house and knock on the door. Mrs. Bascom answers.

"Hi, kids," she says. "What's going on?"

"Is Mr. Bascom home?" Sam asks.

"No," Mrs. Bascom says. "He's been away all week on a business trip. He'll be back tomorrow, though. Can I help you with something?"

"That's okay," Sam says.

"Did you see what happened to the trees on the edge of the forest?" you ask.

"Sure did. What a shame. No one should treat trees like that," she says.

"Mr. Bascom sometimes cuts down trees for firewood, doesn't he?" Sam asks.

"*Once* he cut down a tree that had been struck by lightning and was about to fall over. Other than that, we have our firewood delivered. He would never cut down a perfectly healthy tree!"

You can tell that Mrs. Bascom is more than a little offended by your questions!

■ Oh, well. That was a dead end. Turn back and try another idea!

7

OPERATION Picture THIS

A map is a great way for a spy on a **recon** mission to send info back to HQ. But if that map fell into enemy hands, there'd be trouble.

Fortunately, there are ways to hide maps so the enemy can't read them. A famous spy named Robert Baden-Powell hid maps in his drawings of leaves and butterflies, as you can see on this page. You can read more about Baden-Powell on page 35. For now, try this operation to make your own *artful* maps!

 = Trench

This leaf sketch is actually a map of enemy trenches.

STUFF YOU'LL NEED

- Plain white paper
- Pencil
- Colored pencils
- An object to hide (optional)

YOUR NETWORK

- Friends to read (and *not* read) your maps

The lines on this butterfly's wings are really a map of an enemy fortress. The spots on the wings show the size and position of guns.

 = Fortress   = Guns

WHAT YOU DO

PART 1: LEAF MAP

1 Draw a simple map of the streets of your neighborhood. The streets are supposed to look like the veins on a leaf, so you might need to adjust their angles a little to make them look more natural.

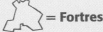

2 Next, draw the outline of a leaf around your map using a pencil. You can make your leaf any shape you want, depending on the shape of your neighborhood. You can see some examples above.

3 Add details to your map using colors normally found on leaves. Use various shades of green, or use autumn colors (red, orange, yellow, and brown). It's up to you. Just be sure to make your details look like natural spots, color patches, or lines on the leaf.

Here are some details you might add to your map:

- **Your home.** Make it look like a spot on the leaf.

- **Other buildings and landmarks.** Draw their shapes roughly, so they look natural.

- **Any ponds, lakes, or rivers in the area.** Make them a different color from the buildings, so that it's clear they're different features.

- **Parks or wooded areas.** Again, use different shading or colors to make these features look different from the others.

4 When you're finished, give the picture to a friend without telling her what you've done. Does she recognize the map of the neighborhood, or does she just see a picture of a leaf?

5 Give your map to another friend, explaining what you've done. Can he identify the location if you give him a **key** to the features?

KEY
- Woods
- Lake
- V Home
- • Friends' Homes
- School

PART 2: BUTTERFLY MAP

Now try making a secret butterfly map to show a friend where to find a hiding place!

1 Sketch the outlines of a building like your home or school.

2 Draw butterfly wings around the building (with the building in the center). Sketch the body of the butterfly right over the center of the building.

3 On the butterfly's wings, draw a spot to show the location of a hiding place outside the building.

4 Using other shapes and colors, draw important landmarks to help your friend find the hiding place.

5 Use any colors you haven't already used to finish decorating the butterfly's wings. Add more lines, shapes, and colors to make the wings look as natural as possible, *without* wrecking your map.

6 Make a key for your map and give the map and key to a friend. Can your friend locate the hiding place? As a test, place an object in the hiding place, and challenge your friend to find it using your map!

KEY
- ● Hiding Place
- ○ Bushes
- School
- Parking lot
- Playground

MORE FROM HEADQUARTERS

1 Think of other pictures you might use to hide a map. Which shapes might work?

2 How about hiding a map in a scribble? Try it. Draw a map of a particular location using only one color, like red. Now, draw other lines and shapes around your map with lots of other colors. The finished product should look like a child's scribbling (or maybe even modern art!). Hand your artwork to a friend, and let her know which color she should look for to find the map. See if she can recreate the map on a separate sheet of paper just by looking at your drawing.

WHAT'S THE SECRET?

Most people see what they expect to see. You presented your friend with a drawing of a butterfly or a leaf—and that's what she saw. She'd have to know the secret to be able to see the hidden map through its disguise.

This is another example of using **camouflage** to hide something. Just like a **ghillie suit** can make a person look like a bush, clever artwork can make a map look like a butterfly, a leaf, a child's scribbles, or whatever else you can imagine.

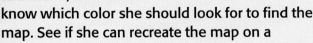

SPYtales

What do butterflies, leaves, and sketchbooks have to do with spying? For Lord Robert Baden-Powell, the answer was...everything!

In the 1890s, Baden-Powell, an English spy, was sent out on recon missions in the Balkans (a region of Eastern Europe). His job was to find out the strengths and weaknesses of military fortresses.

In order to get the information he needed, Baden-Powell disguised himself as a butterfly collector. With his butterfly

Lord Robert Baden-Powell

net in one hand and a sketchbook in the other hand, he looked harmless. But in fact, he was studying and sketching military fortifications.

In a sketch of a butterfly, Baden-Powell hid a map of a fortress and the guns surrounding it. In a sketch of a leaf, he hid a map of trench lines. No one realized that the man with the pretty sketches was a world-class spy!

Besides being a great spy scout, Baden-Powell was also the very first Boy Scout. He founded the Boy Scouts in 1907.

Baden-Powell also hid a map of a fort in a sketch of a moth's head.

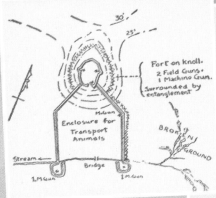

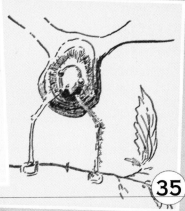

8

OPERATION UnderSea SPY A

Submarines are great vehicles for spies because they're quiet and hard to detect. Submarines have been used to track the movements of enemy ships, and they've helped spies tap into underwater cables and listen to secret conversations.

In this operation, you'll find out how submarines work by building a model of one of the world's first subs, the diving bell. Get ready to plunge in!

STUFF YOU'LL NEED

- A 16-inch (40.5 cm) piece of string
- Tape
- Small rock (should weigh about ½ ounce)
- Plastic cup approximately 3 inches (7.5 cm) tall
- 2 plastic straws with bending tops
- Bathtub

WHAT YOU DO

1 Tape the center of the string securely to the rock.

2 Take both ends of the string and tape them to opposite sides of the outside of the cup so that the rock hangs about 2 inches (5 cm) below the cup's mouth. Make sure that the rock hangs directly below the center of the cup.

3 To keep the strings in place, tape their ends to the base of the cup.

Spy subs don't have to be big like the ones you see in the movies. The Sleeping Beauty submarine shown here was built for just one person! Spies used this craft during the last years of World War II (1939-1945) to sneak up on enemy ships and plant mines (explosives) on them.

4 Insert the non-bending end of one of the straws into the non-bending end of the other straw and tape the two straws together. You now have one long straw.

5 Bend one of the ends of the long straw and stick it into the cup. The end of the straw should reach the bottom of the cup, or very near it. Tape the straw to the inside of the cup.

● TAPE

6 Fill the bathtub with at least 8 inches (20 cm) of water.

7 Place the plastic cup in the water with the rock hanging below it. The cup should float on the surface of the water. You can use the straw to steady the cup if it leans to one side or the other.

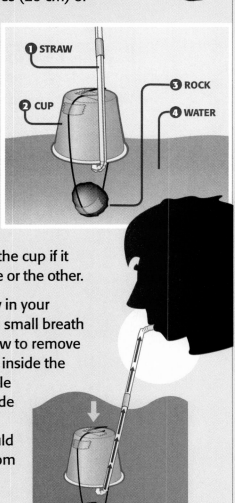

1 STRAW
2 CUP
3 ROCK
4 WATER

8 Put the straw in your mouth. Exhale a small breath through the straw to remove any water that's inside the straw, then inhale the air from inside the cup. Your submarine should sink to the bottom of the tub.

9 Now gently exhale, blowing air into the cup. Your submarine should rise back to the surface. And if you blow enough air into it, your sub should even stand right on the surface of the water!

10 Now try to make your submarine hover underwater. This means that you have to leave just enough air in it to counterbalance the rock's weight and prevent it from dragging the cup to the bottom again.

MORE FROM HEADQUARTERS

Instead of a bathtub, try making a diving tank out of a half-gallon (2-liter) soda bottle. Choose a clear bottle, remove the label, and have a senior spy cut off the top of the bottle. Fill the bottle with about 8 inches of water. Try maneuvering your submarine in this new tank. This time, you'll be able to see the sub rising and falling by looking through the side of the bottle.

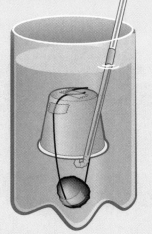

WHAT'S THE SECRET?

In this operation, you worked with *buoyant force* (the force of water pushing upward on an object). To make your sub sink and rise, you made changes to its weight. Turn the page to find out how this works.

HOW THE SUB WORKS

- When you first put your sub in the water, the air inside the cup made it weigh very little, so the buoyant force pushed the sub strongly upward, making it float on the surface.

- When you used the straw to remove the air from the cup, water rushed inside. With more water and less air in the cup, the cup weighed more. The buoyant force decreased, and the sub sank.

- When you used the straw to blow air into the sub, you forced the water out of the cup. The cup became lighter and the buoyant force increased, so your sub rose to the surface.

Real submarines actually have both an inner and outer hull (or frame). The area between these two hulls is called the ballast tank. The tank can be filled with either water or air to make the sub rise or sink— just like your cup sub!

When subs are on the surface of the water, the ballast tanks are filled with air, so the sub floats. In order to submerge, the valves on the top of the sub's ballast tanks are opened, the air inside the tanks escapes, and the tanks fill with water. The sub now weighs more, so it dives deeper into the water. When it's time to rise to the surface again, the sub's tanks are refilled with air.

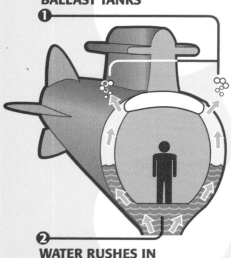

DIVING

AIR RELEASED FROM BALLAST TANKS

① **WATER RUSHES IN** ②

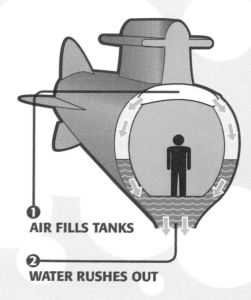

SURFACING

① **AIR FILLS TANKS**

② **WATER RUSHES OUT**

SPYquest

(continued from page 14)

You decide to go with Sam's idea and approach the man from Big Al's Tree Service. When the man turns to greet you, you see that his shirt has a patch that says "Al." This must be Big Al himself!

"Do you know who cut down these trees?" Sam asks.

"No," Al says. "I was just passing by on my way home and stopped to have a look. It's terrible, isn't it?"

"Yeah," you and Sam agree.

"So your company didn't chop the trees down?" Sam asks.

"Are you kidding?" Big Al says. "Whoever cut these trees down did a terrible job and left a big mess. If I'm hired to cut down trees, I clean up the mess. I would never do sloppy work like this."

Well! Sounds like you're barking up the wrong Tree Service!

- This was a dead end. Turn back and try again!

9

OPERATION MEASURE Up

A spy on a **recon** mission is supposed to provide accurate information about everything she sees. When she sees a suspicious building, she needs to record detailed information about its design. But how is she supposed to know how *tall* the building is? She can't just pull out a ruler and measure it! Instead, she'll have to use her math skills to calculate the building's height, with help from an **astrolabe**.

STUFF YOU'LL NEED

- **Astrolabe (see below)**
- **4 x 6-inch index card**
- **Scissors**
- **Pen**
- **Pencil**
- **String**
- **Tape**
- **Penny**
- **Glue**

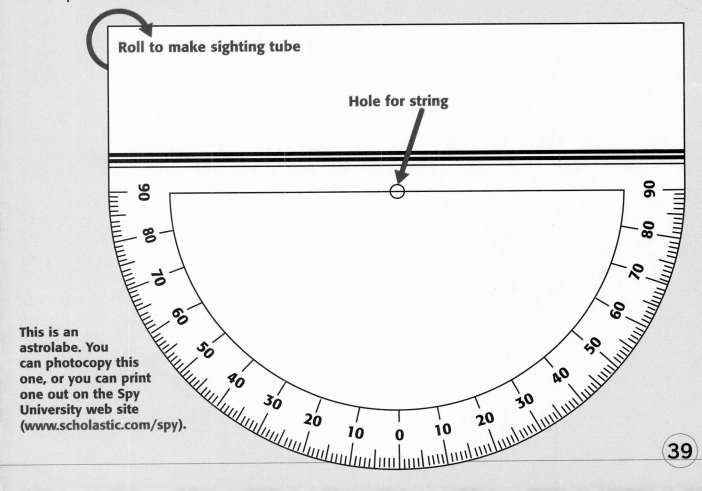

Roll to make sighting tube

Hole for string

This is an astrolabe. You can photocopy this one, or you can print one out on the Spy University web site (www.scholastic.com/spy).

PART 1: MAKE THE ASTROLABE

 1 Make a photocopy of the astrolabe on page 39, or print one out on the Spy University web site (**www.scholastic.com/spy**).

2 Use scissors to cut the astrolabe out.

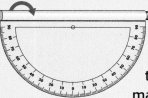

3 Fold the top section of the astrolabe over a pencil and roll it down to the heavy double line to make a tube.

4 Let the tube open slightly so the pencil will slide out, then tape the tube closed.

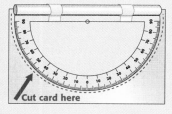

5 Glue the astrolabe to the index card. Cut off the remainder of the index card.

6 Tape a penny to one end of an 8-inch (20 cm) piece of string.

7 With the point of a pen, make a hole for the string in the string hole location on the astrolabe. Thread the string through the hole, then tape the string in place on the back of the astrolabe. Let the rest of the string hang free.

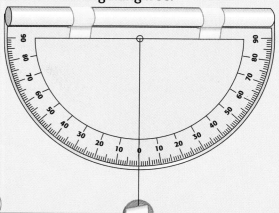

PART 2: FIND THE HEIGHT OF A BUILDING

1 Measure 100 feet (31 m) from the base of the building. One easy way to do this is to measure the length of your foot, and then use your feet to measure the 100 feet. For example, if your foot is 6 inches (15 cm) long, then 100 feet will be 200 heel-to-toe steps away from the building.

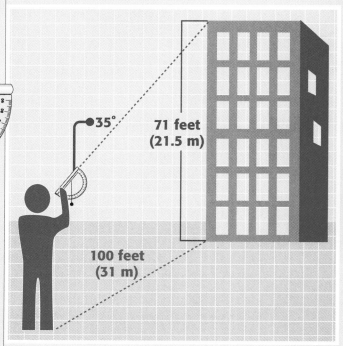

35°

71 feet (21.5 m)

100 feet (31 m)

2 Face the building, and then look at the top of the building through the sighting tube of the astrolabe.

3 Without moving your astrolabe, take a look at the string. It should be touching a number on the astrolabe. That number represents the angle you'll be using to calculate the height of the building.

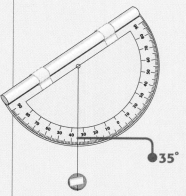

35°

Use the chart on the right to figure out the height of the building. For example, if your astrolabe showed an angle of 35 degrees, the height of the building would be 71 feet (21.5 m).

ANGLE (IN DEGREES)	HEIGHT OF BUILDING	
5°	9 feet	(2.7 m)
10°	18 feet	(5.4 m)
15°	27 feet	(8.2 m)
20°	37 feet	(11.2 m)
25°	47 feet	(14.4 m)
30°	59 feet	(17.8 m)
35°	71 feet	(21.5 m)
40°	85 feet	(25.8 m)
45°	102 feet	(31 m)
50°	121 feet	(36.7 m)
55°	145 feet	(43.9 m)
60°	176 feet	(53.3 m)
65°	217 feet	(65.9 m)
70°	279 feet	(84.5 m)
75°	379 feet	(114.8 m)

MORE FROM HEADQUARTERS

Try calculating the height of other things in your neighborhood, such as your school, a tall tree in the park, or a flagpole.

WHAT'S THE SECRET?

Did you think spies needed to know math? Surprise! In this operation, you used a kind of math called *trigonometry* to find the height of a building without actually measuring it. Trigonometry is the study of the relationships among the sides and angles of triangles. You'll probably take trigonometry (or "trig" for short) in high school. Trigonometry can help you find the height of a mountain, the width of a river, or the length of a train without directly measuring them.

SPYquest

(continued from page 14)

As you watch, the guy from Big Al's Tree Service gets back into his truck and drives off.

"I hope we didn't make a big mistake," Sam says.

Looking around, you notice that one of Sam's neighbors has come out on his porch and is looking in the direction of the cut-down trees.

"Who's that?" you ask Sam.

"That's Mr. Glover," says Sam.

"What do you know about him?" you ask.

"Not much," Sam says. "He keeps to himself."

You watch for a while as Mr. Glover sits on his porch. The sun is setting, and it's about time to shut down your observation post for the night.

"Let's go talk to Mr. Glover," you say. "He might have seen what went on yesterday."

You approach Mr. Glover and find him sitting in a large chair, drinking a cup of tea. You ask him if he has any idea what happened to the trees on the edge of the forest.

"Sorry," Mr. Glover says. "I can't help you there. I don't go near that forest."

"So you didn't see or hear anything going on down there yesterday?"

"Nope," Mr. Glover says. "I'm hard of hearing, so it's not likely I'd hear a chain saw in the distance! Now if you'll excuse me, I'd like to drink my tea before it gets cold, and I'd like to enjoy the sunset before it's over."

You turn to see the sun dipping down below the hills in the distance. You have to admit, it's a beautiful sight.

"Sorry to bother you," Sam says as you turn and walk away, leaving Mr. Glover to his sunset.

"I think we can solve this case pretty quickly," you say.

"I agree," Sam says. "We just have to call Big Al's Tree Service."

You smile. What are you going to do?

■ If you plan to call Big Al's Tree Service, turn to **page 24**.

■ If you think you should talk to Mr. Glover again, turn to **page 48**.

10

What's the best way to get a secret past the enemy? You can use a **code** or a **cipher**, like the Caesar cipher from your *Trainee Handbook*. Or you can hide a secret map in a picture, like you did in **Operation Picture This**. But why not combine these two ideas and use a picture to send a coded message? After all, who would suspect your drawing was a secret code?

STUFF YOU'LL NEED

- **Pencil and paper**
- **Colored pencils**

YOUR NETWORK

- **A friend to decode your message**

WHAT YOU DO

1 Write a simple message that you'd like to encode. Let's say you want to let your friend know when to meet you to start a new spy mission. Your message might read, "Meet at four."

2 Use the grid on the right to encode your message. Each letter is represented by a pair of numbers, like a **map reference**. For example, the letter M is **1,3**. The first number comes from the top row of the grid (directly above the letter M), and the second number comes from the column on the left side of the grid (directly across from the letter M). For each letter in your message, follow this process to get a pair of numbers.

	1	2	3	4	5	6
1	A	B	C	D	E	F
2	G	H	I	J	K	L
3	M	N	O	P	Q	R
4	S	T	U	V	W	X
5	Y	Z				

3 Write out your message in code, putting each word on a separate line. For example, the message "Meet at four" would look like this:

1,3 5,1 5,1 2,4 (Meet)

1,1 2,4 (at)

6,1 3,3 3,4 6,3 (four)

4 Now you're going to turn your letters into apple trees, so you can hide them in a picture. On a new sheet of paper, draw a row of trees along the top of the page to represent the first word in the message. In our example, there are four trees to represent the first word, "Meet." The row doesn't have to be perfectly straight.